Little Stars

Little Stars BMX Bikes

Taylor Farley

A Crabtree Seedlings Book

Crabtree Publishing
crabtreebooks.com

Check out my bike!

POWSEY
POWSEY

It is a **BMX** bike.

ROLLERBLADE

NEW ATHLETIC
SINCE 2005
New Athletic

People use BMX bikes to do **tricks**.

This trick is called a **manual**.

This trick is called an **endo**.

Big kids use the pegs to do **grinds**.

peg

helmet

I wear a helmet.

I ride at the skatepark.

I like to use the ramps.

ramp

One day, I want to ride at the **X-Games**.

GAMES

Glossary

BMX (BEE-em-ex):
BMX is short for bicycle motocross. BMX bikes are off-road sport bicycles used for racing and stunt riding.

endo (EN-doh): An endo is a trick where the rider uses the front brake to balance the bike on its front wheel only.

grinds (GRYNDZ): Grinds are performed using the bike pegs to slide along metal rails or concrete ledges.

manual (MAN-yoo-uhl): A manual is a trick where the rider moves forward, balancing on the back wheel only.

tricks (TRIX): Tricks are clever moves using the bike that take practice and skill.

X-Games (EX-gaymz): X-Games is an extreme sports event that happens once a year and is shown on the television.

Index

School-to-Home Support for Caregivers and Teachers

Crabtree Seedlings books help children grow by letting them practice reading. Here are a few guiding questions to help the reader build his or her comprehension skills. Possible answers are included.

Before Reading

- **What do I think this book is about?** I think this book is about biking tricks, like the picture on the cover.
- **What do I want to learn about this topic?** I want to learn about the tricks a rider can do on a BMX bike.

During Reading

- **I wonder why...** I wonder why BMX bikes have small wheels and tall handlebars?
- **What have I learned so far?** I learned about BMX tricks such as the manual, endo, and grind. Sometimes it looks like the bike and rider are flying in the air!

After Reading

- **What details did I learn about this topic?** I learned that BMX riders practice at skateparks. They do tricks on ramps.
- **Write down unfamiliar words and ask questions to help understand their meaning.** I see the word *manual* on page 9 and the word *X-Games* on page 20. The other vocabulary words are listed on pages 22 and 23.

Crabtree Publishing

crabtreebooks.com 800-387-7650

In Canada: We acknowledge the financial support of the Government of Canada through the Canada Book Fund for our publishing activities.

Hardcover 978-1-4271-2975-8
Paperback 978-1-4271-2993-2

Printed in Canada
102024/CP20241002

Published in Canada
Crabtree Publishing
616 Welland Avenue
St. Catharines, Ontario
L2M 5V6

Published in the United States
Crabtree Publishing
347 Fifth Avenue
Suite 1402-145
New York, NY 10016

Written by: Taylor Farley
Print book version produced jointly with Blue Door Education in 2023

Photo Credits: Cover and pages 8, ll, and 14 © Marcel Jancovic; pages 3 and 5 © Yury and Tanya, page 6 © Christian Bertrand, page 13 © homydesign; page 16 and 17 © Nitikorn Poonsiri; page 20 little girl © Purino, X-Games photo © Haslam Photography, x-games banner © RoidRanger All photos from Shutterstock.com except back cover and page 19 © Anatoliy Karlyuk | Dreamstime.com

Library and Archives Canada Cataloguing in Publication
Available at the Library and Archives Canada

Library of Congress Cataloging-in-Publication Data
Available at the Library of Congress